Within The Mind Lantern

Keerti Nair

BookLeaf Publishing
India | USA | UK

Made with ❤ on the BookLeaf Publishing Platform
www.bookleafpub.in
www.bookleafpub.com

Dedication

To my folks who have nurtured my soul and shaped my journey so far—

My Amma and Accha, my younger Sister and Brother-in-law, my Husband and my two lovely Sons. Hope someday, my Niece who is too young to be aware of this, will be able to look at my book with awe and pride.

To all my friends and acquaintances who have crossed paths and enriched my life with their presence and wisdom.

Most especially, in the loving memory of the best friend I have ever had and will never have—Priya.

This book is a tribute to the complexities and beauty of human life and its capacity to observe the nuances, introspection, growth, love, and transformation.

May this anthology of poems inspire you to reflect, grow, and cherish the moments of your life that make life worth living.

Acknowledgments

I wish to thank Team BookLeaf for coming up with this brilliant thought of a 21-day writing challenge. I am sure this initiative has given wings to many amateur writers like me, who thought writing and publishing books was reserved for literary wizards who were born into some magic world of literature.

Special thanks to my fourteen-year-old son, Vivaan, who has been the only human I have shared my drafts and random thoughts with during this sudden but thrilling journey of writing poems that I embarked on. He has been so easy to please, yet he had such a profound impact on me, as he was always encouraging and motivating with his words about my thoughts and my literary prowess. Love you.

My younger one, who is six, Reyaan, was a witness to some of the brainstorming and research I have had in giving finishing touches to the poems. One day, he curiously asked, "Amma, what are you doing?" I said I was writing a book; he was sweet and quick to get a few pages he had, folded them to make a booklet out of it, and gave it to me to make a book. Love you.

And a big shout-out to my husband, Ajay, who was very supportive and understanding as always. Thank you for holding the fort when I was immersed in writing this book. Love you.

I would like to take this opportunity to pat on my back for achieving this feat which even few months ago seemed distant. Lastly, I thoroughly enjoyed the ideation and designing of my book cover from scratch as well as a few illustrations by me that you will see in the poems.

Preface

'Within the Mind Lantern' is an introspective collection of poems that delves into the complexities of the human experience. Through lyrical language and evocative imagery, these poems are intended to navigate the inner workings of the mind, exploring themes of 1) Nostalgia and Memories, 2) Love, Family & Relations, 3) Nature, Life & Metaphors, and lastly 4) Personal Growth & Inspiration.

With a gentle yet persistent gaze, the poet illuminates the darkest corners of the mind, revealing the intricate web of emotions, thoughts, and memories that shape each of us. From the whispers of the subconscious to the radiant glow of hope and resilience, these poems invite the reader to embark on a journey of introspection and exploration.

'Within the Mind Lantern' is the poet's tribute to the transformative power of poetry, offering a hideout for those seeking solace, guidance, and connection. As you step into the gentle flow of these poems, may you find a reflection of your own journey, and may the words illuminate the path ahead with the gentle warmth of understanding and hope.

Table of Contents

Nostalgia and Memories

(To Cherish)

What's in a Name?

© Illustration by Keerti Nair

A chance encounter, a fleeting meet,
On a train, where lives intersect, brief
and sweet.

Years have passed, yet memories
remain,
Faded faces, but emotions still sustain.

I wonder why this moment stays so
bright,
Giving a fresh feel, despite time's
passing light.

The refreshing, mild smell of his
perfume,
still strongly ingrained,
The strange familiarity, making it so
hard to refrain.

But one question lingers: I wonder and
regret,
Why didn't we exchange our numbers
or names,
Did we just forget?

What if we had a chance, to be thick as
soulmates,
or there would have been more to why
we met.

Can still hear the echoes of laughter, as
I recall that day,
we bonded so quickly, as if we'd
conquer the world in a sway.

Well! Now that I remember,
he must be 10ish, and I was just 8. In
our innocent gaze,
we didn't need phone numbers or
names
For back then, living in the moment,
was all that was to the game.
After all, “What's in a name?” said
Shakespeare, the great!

Though names were unknown, fond
memories remain,
like short and sweet journeys of a train,
For some stories ought to be simple
and plain.

Back to Being

If only I had a superpower,
I'd relive life, again and over.

Only this time, few things not same as ever,
As time waits for none and never.

For now, I know, why and what of my life little better,
Only purpose is to keep becoming a better version of you forever.

In this process, if I discover my dream
and superpower,
Bit by bit, it's okay—I'm lucky,
Though I may not realize it altogether.

For all the places that seemed bigger,
All the things that seemed mightier,
I'd relive life for the smallest things
that made me happier.

Though short and sweet, I'd love,
Going back to being a child again,
Cause who needs the long and bitter
pain.

Sour Candies

© Illustration by Keerti Nair

Reminding us of our childhood days,
When we were a bit naughty and full of
life in playful ways.

They come in various sizes and shapes,
Vivid colors, sour & sweet bites that
our taste buds escape.

Tucked in a perky wrapper so bright,

That served as makeshift dolls of paper,
a pure delight.

Brought a smile on our tired faces to
see,
Innocently carefree, with no pressure
and glee.

As we grow up and become mommies
and daddies too,
These childhood memories become our
sour candies, sweet and true.

Bringing a smile to our tired old faces,
a nostalgic sigh,
Reminding us to cherish the moments
before we say goodbye.

Memories

In the mirror, a little girl gazes,
Dreamy eyed, in a world of her own.
Pretending to be a star, giving
interviews,
In her kingdom, she reigns alone.

Summers filled with endless joy,
Holidays, trains to hometowns afar,
Playing with friends in the scorching
noon,
Running wild, under the sun's bright
star.

Puppies, mud, and plants her
companions,
Chameleons changing colors,
She watched with curious eyes.
Watering plants, cycling around,
Waiting for the ice candy cart's
surprise.

Evenings painted with syrupy hues,
Ice candies in flavors so bright,
Children's laughter, a symphony,
In the warm, fading light.

One day, the lights went out,
Ghost stories whispered in the dark,
Screams and giggles filled the air,
As shadows danced, leaving a mark.

First rains brought a different thrill,
Petrichor rising from the earth,
Dancing in the droplets' embrace,

Moments of pure, unfiltered mirth.

Nostalgia wraps these memories tight,
A warm blanket on a chilly night,
A dreamy child, now grown and wise,
She still finds magic,
Through her mind's eyes.

Have you seen it?

Have you seen it?
That sunlight that covered my
childhood home,
Making the plant fence shine bright
and green?

Have you seen it?
That mud that shined red and familiar?
Those cute little squirrel families
running up and down?
The excitement that came with the first
rain,
building mud castles with friends
together?

Those puppies, all cuddly and warm,
Waiting to be picked up and snuggled?

Have you seen it?
That scary thunderstorm, the trees
dancing to the wind?
That special tree that stood tall and
stout,
Giving shade to my little den, my
home?

Can you bring it to me?
The stomach full of laughs with friends,
The endless running on bare feet on the
warm road?
The star-lit nights and sleeping out
wide and open?

They say, Home is where the heart is,
Have you seen where my heart is?
For I haven't felt it beat off late.

Nostalgia (Moments)

Summer afternoons at Grandma's
house,
As a warm breeze whispers secrets.

Neighborhood streets, where freedom
calls,
Echoes of laughter and wildflowers on
the wall.

Bicycles and dreams, a carefree ride,
Childhood's joy, where hearts full of
wonder reside.

Siblings' giggles, memories to be told,
Family trips and winding paths unfold.

Songs and stories, a journey through
the night,
Stars above, as guiding light.

Sleepovers and secrets, whispers in the
dark,
Friendship's magic, a beacon in the
heart.

Mother's hands, recipes made with
love,
Flavors blend, and aromas rise above.

Attic hideaways, where books come
alive,
Dusty trunks, where forgotten stories
thrive.

High school memories, growth and
truth,
Friendships forged, footsteps bold and
new.

The thrill of love, the pain of heartache
too,
Lessons learnt, memories forever true.

Life's mysteries, love's complexities,
explored,
A safe haven, where moments are
adored and wisdom gained.

Love, Family & Relations

(To Learn)

Deep Conversations

© Illustration by Keerti Nair

Deep conversations with your-kind-a spirits, be like...
A therapy for the soul, where thoughts can freely roam,
the real you rediscovered, like a long-forgotten home.

Like a soothing cup of tea on a weary day,
its warmth helping you chase the blues away.

Like a gentle foot massage after a tiring leg day,
soothing you through the pain.

A cozy TV night after a study's grind,
leaving all the worries behind...

Deep conversations with your-kind-a spirits, be like...

Autumn leaves on a windy day,
a comfortable stillness, giving you solace.

Like a gentle summer rain,
the sweet scent of mud, feeling earthy and divine.

Like a warm blanket on a cold winter night,
that wraps you in its woven threads of gentle care.

Deep conversations with your-kind-a
spirits, are like...
A tight hug from a loved one,
a sense of belonging, that forever
clings.

Reclining Chair

© Illustration by Keerti Nair

Unaware I was... In the midst of
confusion...
about the righteousness of my decision.

After few days, got my answer,
In a way that would amaze,
He chose a song to sing for me...
The song he chose, was special to me,
since the time I had my senses.

The moment he sang...
I knew it all for once, like a big bang...
As if a message out and loud
from the almighty we call 'GOD'...
That was the moment I still am shaken
for I always knew... miracles do
happen!

There I was a few days later...
Committed to a man... strange yet
familiar
cause I always knew him...
Since long in my imaginations!

After almost a year of being together
Despite conflicts, and all the pain...
My heart reckons to commit once
again...
To a man, now known yet in many
ways strange...

cause there was a lot to discover with
passing age.

Differences... and verbal spats...
were bound to occur... for if not that...
we would be called no humans.

The only prayer I had as years went by
may the Almighty give us the
strength...
to forget and forgive...
for there are a number of lovely
things...
happening around... and between us!

Our every day and night together...
our social life together...
sharing of thoughts... joys and
sorrows...
smallest of appreciations and
criticisms...

sharing of responsibilities... and the
masti times...
the house we live... the home we
make...
the bed we share... the love we make...
hugs we exchange, kisses we give...
caring and daring for each other...
even that sweet fight for the good sake
of each other!

May God bless us... with patience...
never-ending curiosity to understand
the other...
ability to prioritize the right things in
life...
face and cross all the hurdles together...
I wish to assure him... I shall try...
and try to make our journey a
pleasurable one...
worth reliving... in our older days...
sitting back on a reclining chair!

Love

When love's pure flame, a soul desires,
Flickers dim, or never truly fires,
A heart, once full, now empty lies,
A life, a journey, through loveless skies.

A yearning deep, a hollowed space,
Echoes whispers of a love's sweet face,
A soul, a search, for what could be,
A heart, a heavy, longing sea.

A smile, a facade, a brave disguise,
Conceals the pain, the tears, the sighs,
A life, a performance, on a stage,
A heart, a heavy, hidden cage.

Self-worth, a question, a nagging fear,
Am I enough, or always near?
A mind, a maze, of uncertain thoughts,
A heart, a fragile, shattered fault.

Yet, still she rises, still she stands,
A phoenix, from the ashes of her plans,
A life, a journey, through trials and
strife,
A heart, a resilient beating life.

For even in the darkness, a spark
remains,
A light, a beacon, that guides her pains,
A hopeful heart, with beating drums,
A love, a dream, that still she feels.

Family Traditions

© Illustration by Keerti Nair

We gather around, as a family that's
tight,
Sharing stories, laughter, and delight.

Our traditions bind us, year by year,
A sense of home, that's always near.

In childhood's eyes, these moments shine,
Memories made, that forever are mine.

The smell of treats, the taste of food so fine,
Homemade delights, that are always so divine.

Board games scattered, laughter loud and free,
Inside jokes shared, memories made with glee.

We play and giggle, our spirits high,
A family's love, that touches the sky.

As we grow up, these moments stay,
A connection so strong, that guides our way.

We pass down tales, and recipes too,

A family legacy, that's forever true.

But when we're apart, nostalgia creeps,
Memories of joy, that softly seep.

We miss the warmth, the love, and the lights,
Of family gatherings, or special nights!

For Granted

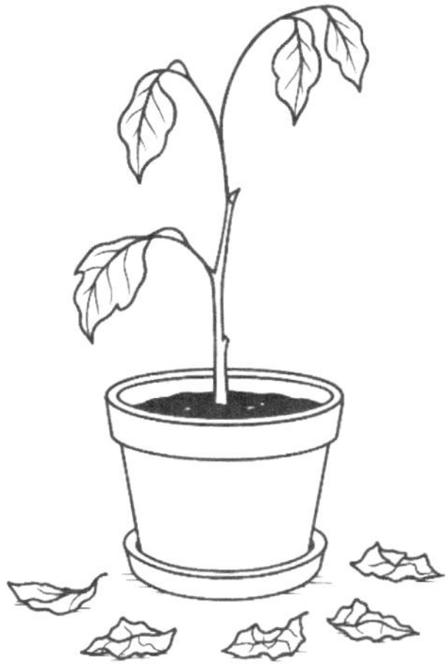

© Illustration by Keerti Nair

It is an endless wait...
A cycle of hopes and disappointments,
Stuck in a chain of heartbreaks.

It is an endless chatter...
a series of talks, expectations, and
emotions,
Lost in a loop of unmet needs.

It is a heap of endless tries...
To make it work, happen, and succeed,
Choked under a lump of wasted effort.

A voice that's ignored...
A cry that is trivial...
Sincerity that no one needed...

A soul that is slowly eroding...
A light that is fading...
A love that once shone,
disappeared.
And that, my friend,
Is a story of being taken...
For granted!

Overhyped

© Illustration by Keerti Nair

Love and wine are overhyped.
since the good old ancient times,
"Like a fine wine!" they say,
but what is the cost?
What is wine? Just yeast feces in a fruit juice!

In the process of making wine,
The grapes lose their form, their shine.

No one talks about the sediments that settle,
The turmoil behind, unseen and forgotten.

Bottled up nicely, put up on a show,
With fine packaging, left to grow old.

As it is, love's a complex, messy thing,
full of contradictions, full of sting.

But still, we seek it; still we strive,
for that fleeting, elusive high!

Void

She was frivolous and timid,
Childlike yet matured,
Taught me to have senseless fun,
And the value of forgiveness.

In her own unique way, she would defy,
Stereotypes and expectations high
Like a tomboy, with a heart so bold
Yet full of love and care.

With a laughter that was contagious
and free
She taught me to laugh at myself,
To be wild and carefree.
Raw and honest, she was the kind I
liked,
A woman supporting woman types.

She told me my worth, yet called me
filmy,
Admired my beauty, criticized my
stupidity.

Sharing our joys, our tears and fears
And listening to each other's talks,
through all the years
We made plans to grow old together,
Getting her son married to my
daughter.

She was gone too soon, ignored and
scarred.

Her soul, still yearning for a warm,
loving hug,
Best friend for life, that I ever had,
One that I will now never have,
left behind a big void.

A Girl

A girl walks, with heart pure and naive,
Through life's journey,
with a steady aim,
To grow, to learn, to be more true,
A better version, of herself anew.

She faces trials, with courage bold,
And rises strong, with a heart of gold,
Her spirit, unbroken, her will, a flame,
Guiding her on, through life's joys and
pains.

With every step, she finds her ground,
And with each fall, she rises sound,

Her mind, a garden, where wisdom
grows,
And her heart, a sanctuary, where love
glows.

She walks, with patience, and a gentle
pace,
And finds her strength, in every place,
Her soul, a canvas, where life's art is
told,
A masterpiece of a story, yet to unfold.

In her journey, she finds her way,
Through life's twists and turns, she
faces each day,
With a heart that's open, and a spirit
that's bright,
She shines, like a star, in the dark of
night.

Nature, Life & Metaphors

(To Reflect)

In and Out of a Fairy Tale

© Illustration by Keerti Nair

She is like a bustling river, on some days,
a force so wild and free.
On others, she is a silent pond,
staring still at life's passing spree.

She is like a lighthouse, guiding the way...
for the lost and weary on certain days.

But on others, like a broken sail,
lost in the storm, with no direction in
hail.

Her mind, on certain days, is brimming
with ideas,
deep and plentiful as ocean tides.
But on other days, unclear and vague,
like a bird flying through the fog's dim
shade.

With child-like excitement,
she embraces life on some days,
but struggles to thrive, exhausted 'on
the base'.

Again, like a warm and cozy sunny day,
She feels alive, for a short while,
Just like a sun-kissed windowpane,
In and out of a fairy tale.

Nature

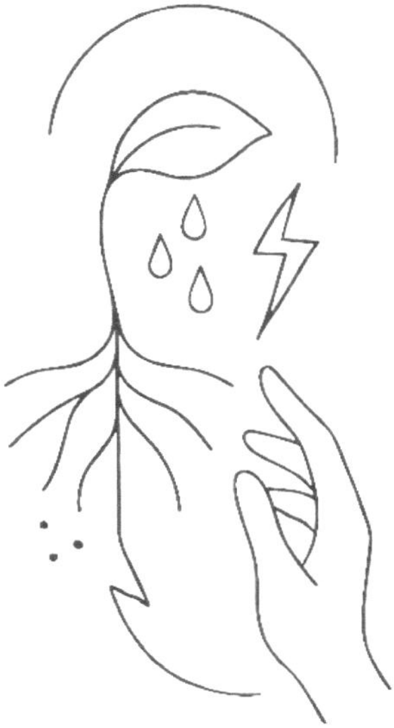

© Illustration by Keerti Nair

Every sprouting leaf, like a newborn,
fresh and vibrant, with skin so pure.

Mud and soil, the very basics,
Helping them heal, nourish, and grow.

Values and habits, like fertilizers,
Helps us shape the quality of our lives.

Water, like relations that bind us all,
if dried up, everything withers and
falls.

Life has purpose and meaning when it
flows,
nourishing roots, and all that grows.

The tiny bugs and mites, like unwanted
thoughts,
can eat away at us, and our inner
strength.

Yet, in nature's wisdom, we find our
way,
to heal, to grow, and to seize the day.

All life's lessons, beautifully captured
in nature's design,
A masterpiece that teaches, heals, and
aligns.

Like a Lotus

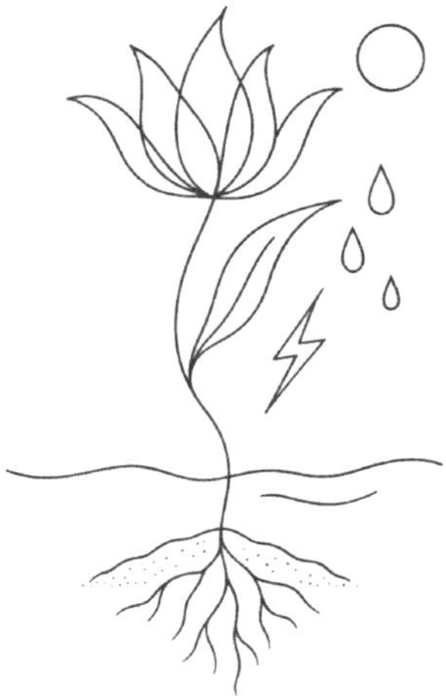

© Illustration by Keerti Nair

Like a lotus blooming in the mud,
The skill of detachment blooms from within,
After thy soul has lived in the deeper corners of the dud.

Like the colorful beauty she is at best,
thy soul shall also glow and shine,
once thou learn to put thy mind at rest.

Like she goes beneath the water at
dusk,
only to reappear for light in the dawn,
Remember, thou shalt too go down
deep through despair,
only to be reborn as tough as a tusk.

Like she stays afloat on the water,
creating shade that keeps the puddles
cooler,
thou shalt also defy all the unwanted
chatter,
Soaring through the gravity of
emotions,
your highest spirit shall bloom.

Firefly

© Illustration by Keerti Nair

Be sincere always, they said,
Is a virtue to have, or so it's led.

Being sincere was all she knew,
Despite her efforts,
deceit came through.

The harder she tried,
her heart did ache,
Tears fell like rain,
her soul would shake.

Too late, she realized.
sincerity's might,
Was it all just overhyped?

At times, she felt lost, left behind,
Wondering if she'd missed life's shine.

Too much of anything is a poison, they say,
A naive girl, head held high,
But with a heart full of gray,
Never knew there needs to be paid a price,
For being too good, too nice!

Like a firefly, shining bright and free,
She thought she'd live forever,
wild and carefree.

She had imagined to be invested full,
Nothing less, no... never!

She learned the hard way,
But finally, made a foray,
Into a world of stray,
Where now she could just be,
But oh, so ready to slay!

Rains and the Soil

© Illustration by Keerti Nair

Rain, nature's precious gift,
Whose beauty goes beyond words' lift.

Its splendor so captivating,
Each drop like diamonds and pearls
sparkling.

It brings a symphony of purity, with
each drop,
Touching the earth, making it come
alive with hope.

Dressed up in the hues of green,
With the scent of damp soil, the earth
begins to grin.

Every time one gazes upon the beauty
of rain-soaked earth,
feels like senses taking rebirth.

Humans are lost in higher pursuits,
Not knowing, here lies the secret of
life,
A mystery that one seeks every day and
night.

Rainbows

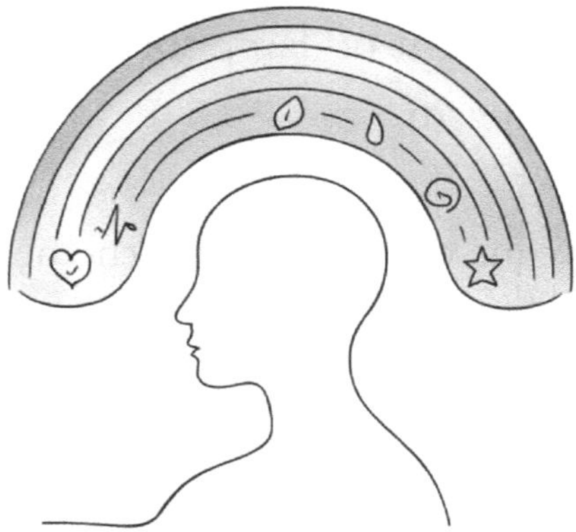

© Illustration by Keerti Nair

Rainbows paint the sky with emotions true,
Each color a feeling, that's real and new.

Red's the spark that sets our hearts aglow,
A flame that burns with passion, and a love that grows.

Orange is warmth, a feeling that's real,
A sense of comfort, that we all can feel.

Yellow's the sunshine, that brightens up our day,
A color of hope, that never fades away.

Green's the calm, that soothes our soul,
A sense of peace, that makes us whole.

Blue's the trust... that we hold dear,
A feeling of loyalty, that's always near.

Indigo's the mystery, that we can't define,
A sense of wonder, that's always on our mind.

Violet's the magic, that we can't ignore,
A sense of enchantment that we adore.

Rainbows are emotions, that we all can see,
A reflection of feelings, that are real to me.

Riddle

© Illustration by Keerti Nair

What a strange riddle is this life,
Oh, my almighty, please resolve this
plight.

Sometimes, even amidst the crowd,
I find myself lonely as a scout.
Then why, in solitude, do I sense
someone's presence unknown?

Sometimes, I deeply understand the
depths of relations...
Then why, at times, do I feel estranged
from my own self?

Sometimes, even my loved ones seem
like strangers to me...
Then why, at times, do strangers feel
like family?

Sometimes, it takes years to
understand people...
Then how, in mere moments, do I grasp
someone's soul?

What a strange riddle is this life...
Oh my almighty, please resolve this
plight.

Butterfly

Like a butterfly in its cocoon,
I am in the early stages of life,
Still unfolding...

As a child, I had thought...
Growing up would make me old.

But now, emerged like a fly,
I see this as just the beginning of it all!

Like a Diamond

© Illustration by Keerti Nair

She was a girl, with a heart full of fire,
A spark that ignited, a flame that aspired,
To be more, to do more, to shine so bright,
But the world told her to dim her light.

She grew, and her spirit, began to unfold,

A woman emerged, with a strength to behold,
She learned to multitask, to juggle, and to care,
For others' needs, while still nurturing her own.

Motherhood arrived, and with it, a new test,
To balance love and discipline and do her best,
To raise tiny humans, with hearts and minds so pure,
And guide them through life, with a love that's strong and sure.

But the world still whispered, of expectations and roles,
Of what a woman should be, and how she should unfold,
To be soft, to be gentle, to be submissive and meek,

But she refused to be bound by these
narrow unique.

She worked on herself, through every
trial and strife,
She honed her skills, and sharpened her
life,
She became a warrior, with a heart of
gold,
Tough on her loved ones, to help them
grow bold.

She pushed and she pulled, with a love
that's true,
To help them become, the best version
of themselves anew,
And though the world judged her, for
her strength and her might,
She stood tall and proud, in the light of
her own sight.

And when her journey ended, and her
final breath was taken,
Her legacy remained, a testament to
her unspoken,
For she was a woman, who lived life on
her own terms,
A force of nature, who burned with
fire,
To be beautiful and bold as a diamond.

Evolution of Dreams

© Illustration by Keerti Nair

In childhood's sleep, where dreams
dance and play,
It's a world of wonder, in a fantasy way.

No boundaries, no fears, just pure
delight,
A magical realm, where dreams take
flight.

As teens, we daydream, lost in thoughts,
Escaping reality, where we feel often caught.

The world outside, we don't understand,
So, we dream of an escape, to a better land.

In our youth in 20s and 30s, new dreams take shape,
Aspirations rise, with a burning ache.

We dream big, of greatness and fame,
Our ambitions soar, with an endless flame.

But life's harsh realities, soon set in,
The ups and downs, the struggles within.

We learn to temper, our lofty goals,
And find that dreams can be more
than just roles.

As we grow older, in our 40s and 50s,
When we've lived and learned,
Faced our fears, and our hearts have
yearned.

We realize now, dreams don't have to
be grand,
They can be simple yet still make a
stand.

We find the courage, to take a step
ahead,
To chase our dreams, with a heart that's
fed.

No longer bound, by fear or clout,
We make our dreams real, without a
doubt.

Summers

© Illustration by Keerti Nair

Summer's warmth brings back
memories old,
Of carefree days, when youth was bold.
No worries creased our brows,
Just laughter, play, and sun-kissed
vows.
We'd chase the ice cream man, with
coins in hand,
And savor the candies, dripping with
sweetness grand.

Mangoes ripe, a taste of heaven's
delight,
Stolen moments of childhood's pure
light.
We'd wear our favorite dresses, light
and free,
And dance in the sprinklers, wild and
carefree.

Buttermilk and lemon juice, a
refreshing treat,
Summer's simple joys our hearts would
greet.
Those endless days, of sun and fun,
Are now just memories, forever young.

We'd run and play, with abandon and
glee,
Summer's magic, a nostalgia for me.
As an adult, I look back in time,

And cherish those moments, so pure and divine.

Though life's responsibilities, have taken their toll,
Summer's warmth still brings a smile to my soul.
The smell of mangoes, the taste of ice cream,
Transports me back to a simpler dream.

Take me to a time when laughter, was the only sound,
And summer's joy was all around.

Tree that stands tall

© Illustration by Keerti Nair

A tree stands tall, through wind and rain,
Its roots go deep; its spirit remains.

It bends and flexes; it adapts to change,
And still it stands, with branches arranged.

In harsh weather, it finds a way,
To weather the storm and seize the day.

Its strength is not in being rigid and strong,
But in being flexible and moving along.

It learns to yield, to let go and sway,
To find its balance, in a new way.

It doesn't resist; it doesn't fight,
It simply adjusts and finds its light.

We are like trees, in our own way,
Our roots are our inner strength, each day.

When life gets tough, and we're bent and worn,
Our resilience helps us, to rise again, reborn.

Just like the tree, we need to bend,
To adapt to challenges and not pretend.

We need to yield, to let go and grow,
To find our balance and learn to show.

Our roots of resilience, help us to
stand,
To weather the storms and take
command.

They help us to grow, to learn, and to
thrive,
To find our strength and stay alive.

But when the mind is brittle, and can't
bend,
It breaks beneath the weight and can't
ascend.

The storms of life, they rage and roar,
And without resilience, we're left on
the forest floor.

Like a tree that's fallen, and won't grow back again,
A mind that gives up, is consumed by pain.

Weeds of doubt and fear, they take their toll,
And termites of negativity, eat away the soul.

The River of Life

© Illustration by Keerti Nair

A river flows, from source to sea,
Ever-changing, yet remaining free.

It winds and turns, through mountains high,
And valleys low, where it meets the sky.

As it flows, it's shaped by every stone,
And every bend, it makes on its own.

It carves its path, through rock and
earth,
And finds its way, through joy and
birth.

We are like rivers, in our own way,
Ever-changing, yet remaining the same.

We flow through life, with twists and
turns,
And shape our path, through every
lesson learnt.

As we journey on, we encounter stones,
That tests our strength and makes us
atone.

We bend and flex; we adapt and grow,
And find our way, through every
challenge we know.

Our journey's not just about the end,
But also, the path that we intend.

The twists and turns, the ups and
downs,
Are all the parts of our life profound?

We discover new depths within
ourselves,
And learn to navigate through life's
wealth.

We find our strengths, and face our
fears,
And grow into the person we are
meant to be, through the years.

But when a river's flow is stopped or
slow,
It becomes stagnant and starts to go
low.

The water gets stale, and starts to
decay,
And the life that once thrived within
us, begins to fade away.

The healing of a dawn

© Illustration by Keerti Nair

The fresh dew drops,
like diamonds bright,
Adorning the leaves,
in morning's first light.

The calm whispers,
of chirping birds afar,
Echo through the trees,
like a soothing song.

Snails and slugs,
crawling at their own pace,
Leaving trails behind,
In the morning's quiet space.

Tall trees mildly sway,
their leaves rustle and play,
Dancing to the breeze,
in a gentle way.

The world awakens,
slow and serene,
As for morning's beauty,
is revealed unseen.

The dawn's healing touch,
brings life new,
A peaceful beginning,
for me and you.

Personal Growth & Inspiration

(To Grow)

The Little Big Things

© Illustration by Keerti Nair

The world talks about big houses you own,
Big paychecks you draw,
The big projects you are working on.

Little do they know of, the small habits you form,
Small gestures you do,
Taking care of people around you.

Small words you keep to not break
their hearts,
While there is a constant rush to excel
in life's every part.

It's essential to take a pause,
To notice the little things that go on
behind,
Every big achievement, every success
that's one of a kind.

Started out with a small thought, small
habits that grew,
Helping them achieve what seemed
impossible, yet came true.
With patience, kindness, and
persistence, they paved their way,
It is these small things that make life's
journey worthwhile in the end.

Self Doubt

Oh, dear, oh dear... why do you fear?
Why take up roles you think they
expect to hear?
Why hide a part of you that makes
them uncomfortable too?
Why underplay your strengths, to keep
them around you?
Why pretend to be someone you're not,
just so they can feel on the top?

Oh dear, oh dear, for once try living for
you.
For there's no audience to perform,
no human to impress or pursue.
Other than the most special
person—the real you, it's true.
So be brutally honest about who you
are, and let it see through.
Wear what makes you feel like you and
let your spirit glow.
Act like what makes you, you, and let
your heart be free to do.
Do what makes you happy from within
and let your joy shine through.
Not for fake smiles that get clicked,
but for a happiness that's real and deep.

Being yourself doesn't make you bad;
it's just not what you've had.
It's the wrong stories you read and the
little you were told,

It's never too late to rewrite the story
and make it a happier one to be told.
A story of the girl you always secretly
wanted to be.
A boy you were too scared to be, so
you became what was expected to see.

To be your true being,
Is a skill you've forgotten,
But let me remind you, my friend,
that's the only being,
you were truly meant to be, after all!

Failures

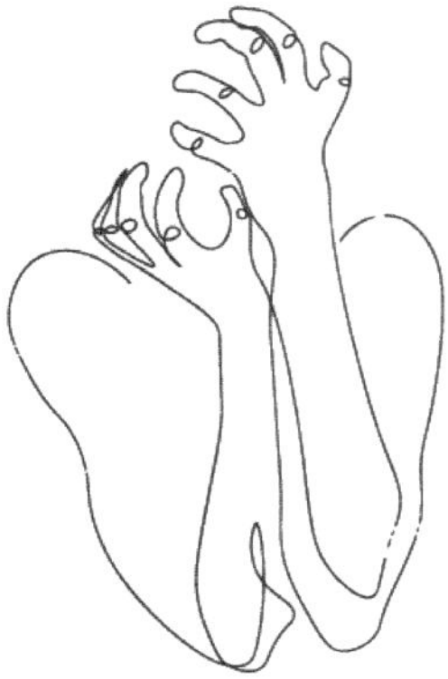

Try, try, and try until you succeed,
For failures are the stepping stones to success.

So much hullabaloo surrounds success,
But sheer silence about the process.

Failures are a shame, or so they claim,
If you succeed, you're in the game, yes, you get all the fame.

But I am no dame,
overnight successes are so lame.

You ought to fall and fail,
get up, keep working at it, still the
same.

Real success is when you learn,
and not what you earn,
Real earning is not the money in your
bank,
It's in the people you inspire and thank,
Laughter and blessings you get,
the hearts you touch,
the warmth your soul begets.

But remember, ain't needed to be a
people pleaser,
Not at the cost of your being,
be the being you aim to be,
That mankind yearns to be with,
In that process of becoming that being,

Be careful you break no hearts,
and do no harm.

Just keep your head down,
Ignore the unavoidable frowns,
For one day shall come,
when you will shine bright and strong.

So be beautiful, be ready,
to be in the world's spotlight!

Slumber

When the soul's flame flickers low,
And life's vibrant hues begin to slow,
A human being may retreat to sleep,
In dormancy's quiet, mystic keep.

Grief's dark shroud may wrap around,
And numb the heart, a heavy mound,
The mind, a maze of pain and fear,

May lose its way and slumber here.

When dreams, like autumn leaves, fall cold,
And hope's bright light begins to unfold,
The heart, a heavy, weary weight,
May succumb to dormancy's dark fate.

Fear's dark specter may loom near,
And paralyze the soul, a frozen fear,
The mind, a prison of anxious thought,
May lock itself away, and slumber brought.

When passions fade, and energy wanes,
And life's demands, like waves, crash and sustain,
The body, mind, and spirit worn,
May surrender to dormancy's quiet morn.

Yet, in this stillness, a chance to renew,
A time for reflection, and dreams
anew,
For in the depths of dormancy's dark
night,
Lies the potential for rebirth's first
light.

True to Oneself

In a world of fleeting moments and curated frames,
It's easy to get caught up in the endless digital games.

Surrounded by the constant hum of social media's sway,
It's tempting to present a perfect picture, every single day.

With AI and algorithms guiding our every move,
It's natural to feel the pressure to constantly improve.

The fear of missing out can be overwhelming at times,
But in the midst of all this noise, it's essential to be true to oneself.

What does it mean to be true to oneself in this digital age?
To find one's own voice, amidst the race of the online stage.

It is a question worth exploring, a journey worth taking,
Discover the beauty of authenticity, and the freedom it awakens.

Don't let the Light Dim

A voice says from within,
Don't let the light dim.

In the darkest corners of my mind,
A flame flickers, a light left behind.

A spark that refuses to fade,
A beacon in the blackest shade.

A voice says from within,
Don't let the light dim.

The shadows creep; they whisper low,
Of fears and doubts that I've yet to
know.

But still I hold on to what's true,
A light that shines, a heart that's new.

A voice says from within,
Don't let the light dim.

In the silence, I hear a voice,
A whisper that makes my heart rejoice.

A call to rise, to shine, to be,
A light that guides, a soul set free.

A voice says from within,
Don't let the light dim.

The world outside may try to break,
My spirit, my will, my heart's ache.

But still I stand, I hold on tight,
A light that burns, a beacon in the
night.

A voice says from within,
Don't let the light dim.

In the darkness, I'll find my way,
Through the shadows, I'll shine my day.

A light that guides, a heart that's true,
A soul that's strong, a spirit anew.

A voice says from within,
Don't let the light dim.

The Next Phase

I think I am ready for the next phase,
like a new chapter of a book,
the next ride from one place to
another,
like travelling into the new world,
unknown streets and new faces that
pass by,
ready to soak in all the sunshine,
that seeps in through the windowpane.

I think I am ready for the next phase,

with a mind full of fears and
uncertainties,
but also hopes and prayers,
with glimpses of happy faces,
laughter, chuckles, and the twinkling
eyes.

I think I am ready for the next phase,
with heart full of pain and hurt,
but also pride and courage,
with emotions like new color shades
taking birth on a palette, white and
clean.

I think I am ready for the next phase,
or maybe it's just a fleeting thought, a
passing feeling,
or am I really ready for the next phase?

Dance

In the realm of existence,
where tasks are defined,
There lies a world of depth,
where true meaning is designed.

A realm where joy resides,
and bliss is revealed,
When creativity flows,
and the heart is healed.

What is an art, you may ask,
with a curious mind?

An expression of thought, feeling, or
emotion aligned.

A shining manifestation of your
creativity,
Through the soul's deep core.
Where imagination knows no bounds,
and beauty is restored.

Dance is a holistic art,
of body, mind, and spirit entwined,
A form of divinity,
when treated with reverence and time.

Yet, like all things in life, it's subject to
misuse and plight,
A reflection of the world's duality,
where good and bad take flight.

No need to convince or fight,
for in coexistence we reside,

Where shadows and light entwine, and
the dance of life abides.

Embracing the paradox,
we find the beauty in the strife,
And in the rhythm of the dance,
we discover the essence of life.

So let us move with intention,
and let our spirits soar,
For in the dance, we find the bliss that
we've been seeking evermore.

With every step, a story's told,
of the human heart's deep core,
A testament to the power of art,
to heal, to inspire, and to restore.

Head Held High

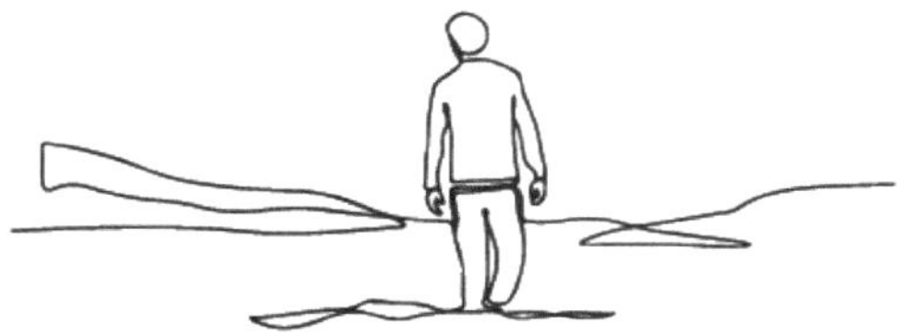

Walk with your head held high,
For you will be able to look,
near and beyond.

Talk with your head held high,
For no matter who it is,
will respect you,
only if you respect yourself.

If someone ignores you,
keep your head held high...
Continue going forward,
For the same person might,
try hard to meet you,
in the journey ahead.

if someone belittles you,
keep your head high...
Walk away far,
for only then they will know,
your real worth and want you.

If someone tries to sabotage you,
keep your head high...
Walk faster, for they,
might fall flat on their feet one day!

If someone imitates you,
smile, keep going with your head held
high,
For they are already inspired by you
and will look up to you!

If someone tries to outshine you
let them do, but remember,
Your sunshine cannot be matched,
by anybody, but only you!

A Woman

She walks the fire, of her own desire,
A path of flames, that fuels her highest
wire.
No fear can stop, her burning soul,
She's driven by passion, to make herself
whole.

She carries the storms, within her
grace,
A wild calm, no one can replace.

She bleeds in silence, she smiles in
pain,
Yet dares to rise, again and again.

Her heart beats strong,
As clear as a drum in the night,
A rhythm that guides her,
through life's darkest fight.

She rises fierce,
with a warrior's cry,
Unbroken and wild,
she faces the sky.

Her mind is a storm,
of thoughts and emotions raw,
A hailstorm of feelings,
that she must learn to draw,
a masterpiece of her own,
A work of beauty,
born from the ashes known.

She's a force of nature,
untamed and free,
A wildflower blooming,
in the darkest sea.

Eternal Love

Finally, she knew how to love,
that love can be eternal.

The eternal love she now felt,
ran deep, beyond explanation.

No one else would understand,
but her love was greater than ever.

Ever and ever, she searched for it,
and finally found it within.

Within her now there was a spark lit,
a spark of self-love she had before
never felt.

For the feeling of self-love,
mattered the most,
as life unfolded, bit by bit.

She yearned for love all her life,
only to discover, late, the truth:
she ought to have loved herself First!

Well, how could one preach what they
don't believe?
Or sell what they don't find worth
themselves?

Inner Gold

A newborn arrives, with a blueprint so fine,
A personality shaped, before a single line.

Parenting's role, often overstated, some say,

For innate character guides us on our way.

Some talented souls, struggle to make their mark,
While others rise, with ease, and a gentle spark.

Destiny's hand, guides us through life's tide,
Where some succeed, with effortless stride.

Yet discipline, persistence, and a positive mind,
Can shape our fate, and make our dreams align.

The best version of our destiny unfolds,
When we work in harmony, with our inner gold.

Within the Mind Lantern

© Illustration by Keerti Nair

Within the Mind Lantern of ours,
is a light so divine and precious.
Illuminating different shades of colors,
It is the guiding light, till we take, last
breath of ours.

We ought to take good care of our
lantern minds,
For it can make or break our lives.
It can turn life into a spectacle, or leave
it a mere mime,
depending on each string of light we
can join.

Let's explore through every shade and
light,
not to forget the in-between spaces.

Let's discover and unravel ourselves,
learn and unlearn, to our heart's
content.

Let's make our mind lantern strong and
wise,
so we can withstand any storm that
shall come and rise,
Keeping our lantern's light forever
alive.